A

GREAT

SIBERIAN

SILENCE

poems

RANDI LEE

ANDERSON

First edition June 2020

Cover design by Aero Gallerie

ISBN 978-1-7352028-0-8 (paperback)
ISBN 978-1-7352028-1-5 (ebook)

Published by Candless Creative
www.candlesscreative.com

To all the beautiful souls I encountered in Russia,
but in a special way to Zhenya,
to Hugues and Anatoly,
and to Father Janez.
All of you, named and unnamed,
have been instruments of immeasurable grace.

CONTENTS

Wondering

Waking

this quiet flame
of homelessness
is burning me
alive

—Katherine MacKenett, "Daily Magnet #215"

A

GREAT

SIBERIAN

SILENCE

URSA MAJOR WAKES IN JANUARY

What stirs, when through whorls of snow
I glimpse memory sluicing past,
stories ended unbegun, a velvet curtain dropped
as I'm standing in the aisle of a dimming opera hall,
wondering where the light, the scenes, the costumes go?
I left the hall for another, blurred,
swaying. As guide, a double-vision of what was,
so swaddled in aching nostalgia it takes on the gloss
of a brown-glass bottom in a bar where the lights
died hours before.

It was life I longed for, life I ran from.

Now winter white is vigor and silence
as I dream behind finger-streaked windows, muttering,
My God, is there life in living?

Someone left a polar bear card with a smile,
no salutation. No one knows what to say anymore.
It's January; I fold my hope and burrow in deep-dark to
     dream.
As a child I named myself winter. Even then
I knew where my visions were born.

WITHERING

THE GHOST LIGHT'S SONG

My dreams were beams in vaulted galleries
where dust motes waltzed and winked
like flakes of sun, and my heart steamed, warm
on a banister.

Hollow-chested, I lingered at windows
and sang with the heart I heard beating—
sun-blinded, bare-breasted, I sank
beneath the sill and wrapped round me
a chrysalis curtain.

In the hollow where my heart lay once,
a light gathers, hardens
and pales.

Now night drips through misted panes
as I become the cobwebbed candle, the friar's lantern
wandering bogs, luring princes
to watery vaults.

As they sink they gurgle their love song:

your dreams were beams in vaulted galleries,
where once we waltzed and winked
like flakes of sun, where once your heart steamed window
    panes

yet dries now, sun-bleached
on a banister.

THE HILL-TOP EXILE, DREAMING STILL

In sight of far-off cupolas flaming in sunrise
I trod on your face in the snow.
The sacred song cleaved to my throat as I held
your nose, crushed sideways
your mouth, stuffed with black earth
your eyes, still and smooth as knobs of ice.

Now I wander, weeping, and hang
my golden bones from birch
and poplar. Tears roll on the heels
and run until the day of return,
until rivulets of salt and blood
crack ice on the river.

Oh forgotten-name, whose music I mourn
forever among these valleys—

you were only breaking through, when I
(gold-blinded) forgot my heel, when I
(sun-inflamed) dashed your face
against time that never was
and never would.

EMPTY PODS

One-thirty in the morning, the tree roots
in my chest. It burrows through throat
and belly, vessel and nerve, feeding on chips of starlight,
tendrils of hope and a dream's afterglow.
When it punctures my eyes, I give in—
the tree knows it's fated to wither,
blacken and collapse, consumed again
by its own hollow core.

Two-thirty in the morning, the lump in my throat
knots, germinates and sprouts, blooming
by dawn. I work my mouth around a nothing-word,
a no-one-word, a syllable that crumbles
to powder the moment it's spoken,
only to germinate again.

At three, I wake, and notice:
what a garden I've made of these.

My vast no-one's-glory, my secret field
of nothing-reaped, my empty pods strewn
about this body, secreting the aroma of a lie
told twenty-seven times—

What a garden of fruitless desires, decaying
at the roots of ripening hours.

LOOK, MY BONES

Look: my bones
are curling like staircases
up my spine.

Without blood
I'm strong and slender.
Without blood
my beauty draws the awe
from your mouth
as she spirals and spins
and gathers all
in her wind. I'm the still,
solid core
when nothing is left.

The bones
crack under your feet,
the beauty
crumbles, but you scale.
Your hand
on my core, you scale
to snow-eyed
peaks where the winds
blow dry
and the sky is silent.
You ask
my face, receive no answer.

Below you,
no way down.

Listen: my bones
were my voice, they spoke
as you climbed.

This is me,
when nothing is left.
This is me,
when at last you wish
to speak.

SELF-PORTRAIT, SPINNING

Mine is not the insanity that marches, muttering
of Waterloo. It huddles in the heart's high tower
weaving visions of sunlight scattered in mirrors.
My foot taps its spinster-song march to someday-glory,
tap-tap as wheel and loom hum refrains to the song

in endless round muttered——*meine Ruh' ist hin*
ist hin ist hin

——and the round resounds in light reflected, refracted
and shattered in shards all congratulating, confirming
one another until they fold on the loom's horizon
to rise again, another false day. Unsinkable.
Iceberg warning ahead; full speed, I spin.

Mine is the insanity that weathers: strap me, and I grow
    stronger
with every squirming feat of resistance required to believe.
The city's unsinkable, founded on patterns and
    perseverance,
repetitive runs carving ruts into time. Longer than Troy
it's stood against you: it demands a subtler horse.

But the queen overthrown from within
invites invasion.

Come, bring your horses and cannons, your icepicks and
    axes,
for I invite defeat—true night in exchange for true day.
With the left side of my mouth I invite you: steal my light,
steal my gold, steal the straw I've hoarded, hoping
some alchemy of the heart might spin something real.

Then I'll wake and weave a new banner, singing hymns
of a humiliated dawn, where we have lost
what we haven't loved, where we now love
what we cannot lose. The tower of the loom sinks blue
beneath the waves; the sun waits there, a second shore.

From here, the iceberg looms.

WEATHERING

DEATH AND PIGEONS AT DAWN

With morning, the pigeon alights by my pillow, bearing
on his wing a tiny death. He shudders it off
in clouds of building-site dust that settle
in the waking eye. Death coos in dreaming ears
before the mouth has a thought to pray.

Around my head my old friend flies, a dream
the dawnlight forgot to chase. He'll come again. I cannot
    catch him
with hands floating far in the deep, where in swells of cold
the dark things rise to nip my fingertips.

I feel it, now. Death burrows deeper, through eardrums
and thick eye jelly as fog rolls up and in,
recoloring all I saw. What was green, now silver-gray.

It was you I saw, last morning: it was sun in my eye
and dew on the lens. A ray through a thin-veined leaf.

I forgot death flies in dreams.

THIS IS ALL I KNOW OF WAR

This is all I know of war:
fire-flowers on a TV screen,
surround-sound chopping of copters,
whining bombs, shuddering earth.
Rat-tat-tat of bullets punching
through speakers, crisp, pristine.

I know pressed uniforms, gleaming
caskets, ladies in pearls, veiled hats
and victory rolls standing, hands
clutching young fatherless sons.

How must it be to write letters
to a fiancé lost at sea, to be unable
to fathom the leagues between you
but to try, late at night, as you wake
open-mouthed, drowning?

How must it be to hear rat-tat-tat
and sand blooming, to see fires unfurling
like petals as your friend's face
crumples beneath?

In those final seconds, knowing
the long wait is over, the tension breaks;
the films can't prepare you for this.

THE MAGDALENE

When truth plucks the beard
of your dream and spits
on its fair face

the sentence of death, what remains
but to hold your tongue, Lamblike,
up winding streets to Golgotha?

Can I wash my hands of the hope,
or must I trail it, wailing
and beating my breast

to the last
drop spilled, the last
gasping offering?

I am the Magdalene, crouching
at the mouth of the tomb,
peering in—asking

what gardener has taken
that once-fair face,
beloved.

What remains to me?
A face I do not recognize,
a friend I cannot hold.

DIPTYCH: A LINE IN THE SNOW

I.

Fresh snow, a girl out dragging a stick —
one long stripe, two small:
an arrow.

Down the sidewalk, again.
Her arrows I follow from sun-scorched dreams
to lines of poplars, slumbering and dark
as a riddle in wood. I cannot hold; the things I carried
fall away with winter twilight.

She cuts the snow, she cuts the line
between me and something other,
now points her stick and says
this is meeting, this is parting—
this point here.

II.

The girl now drags her stick
across the surface of my heart. Three grooves,
one bloody-bright arrow leading me to all the treasures
I hold already, here in black-gloved hands
weighted with riddles.

Here, she says,
at this point here—you've all the beauty
a hundred suns could not outburn.

She drags her stick across my palm
and carves your name, an other's beauty
I cannot hold, I cannot hold,
an arrowed beauty pointing here
to all the treasures holding me.

ONE LAST THING (A SONG FROM THE NORTH COUNTRY)

I no longer ask you to love me—
only turn your bright face to the northwind
I've sent from my pocket (kept there
so long, oh so long!)
and let it blush your cheek once more
for me.

Winds pass, you know;
let this come, let this go.

I no longer ask you to hold the door
or light candles at night (on the sill,
oh too long)—
only raise your bright hands to the stars
I've let fall, the last pennies in my pocket
for you.

Stars burn out, you know;
let this come, let this go.

WONDERING

"THIS QUIET FLAME OF HOMELESSNESS"

For Katherine

I run,
limbs aflame,
heart a coal
incandescent black.

I collapse—

from ashes
I trust.

NOTRE DAME DE PARIS

On this pockmarked road
under stars of crane-lights
and cameras I stand

in a mantle of dusklight,
warm in the core, a luminous
face above—pallid, tranquil as stone

yet alive—
a half-smile hinting
of realms above the dark veil.

SOUL'S NIGHT

For Father Jacques

You wore the soul's night
longer than some
wear their skins.

You showed me a child's wing,
iridescent, fallen from a mountain ash
where it had caught and fluttered for years.
You laid it in my palm, and whispered,
"Remember."

I remember only this—
you wore a heart's face close to your mouth
and incanted in the darkest hours,
hoping it would open
the light we forgot.

GLIMPSE

You tap my heart
till I recall
a time glimpsed overseas:

a dreaming land,
pure poetry—
a secret bower of rain,

the fairy tree,
the late-night tea,
a darkened windowpane—

and early songs
of hidden birds
all lauding mysteries.

BREADCRUMBS

Setting out, no one expected rain.
In sun we held our memories
like marbles, bright and burning
through our pockets,
jeweled breadcrumbs left behind.

But drizzle fell, and torrents followed,
until our pockets sagged
and slapped our anklebones
through darkened lanes, and I,
I looked behind—

a winding trail of marbles,
winking lamps in purple gloom.
My fingers trickled tiny spheres
of lily-white and lion-gold,
so faint a gleam beneath the flood—

and I remembered
how it had been, once:
how it could be, once again.

SEPTEMBER 12

Remember your self, summer voyager:
you're home again in slick black streets
and yellow leaves, the aromatic steam of tea,
the hardcover's crackling spine,
the brilliant, painted, Pushkin *Osen'*—
here's your fire, your hearthside peace.

You are the window-candle,
the guidelight in the northern night,
the place where hurt ones huddle
and dream of things-anew.

WAKING

HONEY FROM NAILS

O Mensch, bewein' dein' Sünde groß.
- from *Matthäus-Passion*, J. S. Bach

Somewhere over the way-up-high,
you dreamt we loved one another.

You drew honey from nails in a tree
while I waltzed on cliffs bestarred with faces

and infinite spaces below your mountain
white with solitude.

You descended
and pierced those stars, squeezed between

to find my soul, bone-thin
and quivering.

A window open;
now, the door—

I clutch at tumbling stars
and slipper my feet to waltz, waltz,

waltz the edge, away from your blazing white mountain,
your honey that tastes of bark and blood.

But tell me, before I waltz out of your
light, is it fire—is it tundra—

can it reach you now, this song?

It's you on my shoulders when I carry
my dreams cross-land; it's you I glimpse

in the whistling snow when love breaks,
when dawn forsakes me at first light.

I listen for your footsteps
crunching the snow—

> *(Erbarme Dich, erbarme*
> *Dich, mein Gott)*

FROZEN RIVER

I glimpse you on the riverside,
a speck amid the snow.

Between us, fields of sharp-edged white.

Between us, spikes in gleaming rows:
shark's teeth and shattered plates.

You cross the jagged fields,
but I can't see you in the glare.
You cross with naked feet—
I glimpse a winding scarlet trail.

Shall I step out now?
Scar my soles?
Like you, I have no shoes.

Shall I meet you on the ice, my friend?
Can the river hold us two?

ON METROS, ETERNITY, AND MOZART

To write about Heaven I had to loop
a Mozart lullaby,

two and a half minutes to lull myself out
of a dry-eyed world of dustworn shoes
and double split shifts, urban exhaust
and late-night sinus drainage,
missed metros and slow-walking couples
taking up the sidewalk with their happiness.

Lifted on waltzing strings,
I hoped to forget (or truly,
remember)

how I saw you in sunbeams and pine,
dipping your hand in a snow-glutted stream
in a spring beyond farewells.
Your eyes spoke of Sunday forever,
of time loose and light

and silence resounding with the Beauty
that struck Salieri between the lines.

That day there will be no lines
of ink (but pure note),
nor lines of the metro
taking me this way, and you that.

(Imagine: time distilled
to a moment, taking up eternity
with its oneness.)

Until then you loop from heart
to head, always two and a half minutes
between your platform and mine.

A SONG OF HEAVIER THINGS

Oh creeping, creeping
seeping feeling, feeling up my legs
and egging down my throat
with a coating of kitchen sink grime—

timing the ticks of the hours
and souring the eyes, the lies
the alibis, tithing to glass-gods
coddling vices, dicing the prices
financing my sins, yes, rotting the loom
and dooming me down,
down,
down.

I need
a good laugh, a long sleep,
vast skies and clear hours,
no screens, no glass-gods
calling me—

I need steam and frost,
birch and stream,
light and shadow dappled.
I need quiet nights and birdsongs.
Honest work, a child's fears.

I need star-speckled nights like jeweled eggs
hollowed out to be filled.

Afloat in comforts, I miss the deep.
I miss the heavier fertile things
that settle, cool at the bottom, enrobed
in creekbed grime. They do not run with the stream,
but the stream draws life from them—
eroding me, enriching you.

But while the waters eddy at my toes and the mud
clings to my ankles and the wind on the face of the waters
slackens—or stills—
I lose sight of the depths and the heavier things
and fear the drowning,
fear the drowning,
fear the murky place where nothing lives
but the *vodyanoi* with his black tail coiling—
feeling up my legs and dooming me down,
down
DOWN…
his eyes dark and hollow, never filled, despite long sleep
and light and shadow dappled
and the laughter that tastes of a child's fears
grown up.

Oh creeping, creeping
seeping coils,
you cannot—you will not—

You lurk behind screens,
coddling vices, dicing the prices,
egging down throats to coat the heart
in kitchen sink grime,
but you will not—

not while the wind is high
and the birch leaves rustle,
calling me, calling me
down
(down,
down...)

DEATH-DANCE IN THE COFFEEHOUSE

Russians, they said, don't believe in silence—
if it's silent, something's wrong. That must be why

I can't write alone in a café corner
without an embassy settling, pigeon-like,

and clearing the silence before them. Something's wrong
with a darkened café, a voiceless corner, a girl too full

of prayer and pu-erh. Let us purge her with chatter and
     cheer,
mementos of a forgetting world. Life is sound—life's a
     shout!

Life is voice, and voices are life! Let us make it so
quickening-loud, we can't hear ourselves dying.

Nor living, either.

In the notebook I hear us all living
as seeds of long memory stir. Life begins here

in silence, in the humming depths of earth.
The Russians used to know. We all knew, once—

until we learned to play the danse macabre
so withering-loud it deafened the soul, darkened the eye

and we couldn't see whose skull we trampled.
But don't pity the skulls—they live. I hear them

chattering my name. From the pounding earth
I'll bless the sound of forgetting and burrow

beneath, to the lost, the silent remembering. Here
life begins again. Let the dance swing on above.

I turn the page.

ACKNOWLEDGMENTS

My deepest thanks to those whose advice and encouragement made these poems, as well as the collection as a whole, better than they would otherwise have been. This means special thanks to Kelsey Peterson, Cassie Mosier, and Erica Anderson, as well as to my poet "pen pals" such as I. Balestri (yes, you, AlwaysRainCheck!) whose poetry and support both inspired me and gave me courage. On this note, I would especially like to acknowledge Katherine MacKenett, our beloved Fridge Poet, whom I hope to meet in person in the next life. Thank you for lighting my way, and thank you for inspiring us with your brief but enchanting poems that brought out the child, the mystic, and the artist in all of us.

RANDI LEE ANDERSON writes, paints, sings, translates, and—for much of the year—teaches English at the university. Her teaching has taken her around the globe, most notably to Novosibirsk, Russia, where she lived and worked for 18 months, learning Russian and writing poetry in her spare time. Her poetry has previously appeared in the speculative literary magazines *Strange Horizons* and *Quantum Fairy Tales*. She now lives in Pennsylvania with her rather spoiled tabby cat Dmitry, also a world traveler.

www.randileeanderson.com